Courage to M.O.V.E.
THE JOURNEYBOOK.....

MAXIMIZING YOUR MOMENTS

OVERCOMING YOUR OBJECTIONS

VALUING YOUR VISION

EMBODYING YOUR EXTRAORDINARY

Ebony Vaughan

Courage to MOVE

Courage to MOVE is a powerful book designed to equip people to gain the character and commitment necessary to obtain their God given dreams and goals. Having courage in our journey through purpose is so important because it enables the development of stamina and resilience in purpose.

Throughout the book, are key strategies, tips and wisdom guaranteed to help the reader to discover and begin to walk in their God given purpose on earth. Purpose is defined by Oxford Languages, "as the reason for which something is done or created or for which something exists." Discovering our purpose has everything to do with each of us discovering our "why" on earth. How many of you have asked God or yourself, "why am I this way?" The answer to this question can only come from the one who made you, your creator. It is my belief that Purpose is something that God has determined and fashioned us for when we were in our mothers womb. I want you to think about that dream, that goal that you just could never shake. Could it be that, that this thing that I have always dreamed of as a child was really a plan that God birthed in me when I was in my mothers womb. Could it be that he fashioned me to fulfill his purpose?

These questions are essential to being able to discover and execute the plan of God for our lives.

As we talked about in the book, M.O.V.E stands for Maximizing Your Moments, Overcoming Your Objections, Valuing Your Vision and Embodying your Extraordinary. This acronym depicts the supernatural journey required in order for us to have the abundant life that God spoke of in John 10:10.

Maximizing your moments has everything to do with us understanding that every moment we are alive is a Gift From God and we are to live it to the fullest. The bible says that our days are numbered, and it becomes our responsibility to be a good steward of the gift of life. According to Oxford Languages, stewardship is defined as the job of supervising or taking care of something, such as an organization or property. God desires us to be good stewards of the time that he has given.

Overcoming your objections speaks to the need for Gods people to challenge their inner self critic and challenge the low esteem and insecurities that life has a way of causing us to develop. One thing that I understand about trauma and tragedy that it has a way of tainting our internal environments causing us to believe that we are what we have been through. Trauma and tragedy has a way of causing us to think low of ourselves and live in internal and external environments of hopelessness and despair. Overcoming objections has everything to do with learning how to create positive and hopeful internal environments that challenges a person to experience renewal and restoration. Renewal causes the people of God to create new paradigms that are in alignment with what God says about them. When we overcome our objections we choose to align our thoughts with the thoughts of God our creator.

Valuing your Vision empowers us to begin to take our dreams and the purpose of God for our lives seriously. I say this because many of us are happy to believe in the pursuits of others even to the point of helping others build, yet we fail to believe in our own dreams and goals. When we value our vision, we give ourselves permission to invest in our selves. Investing in ourselves, no longer is a bad word or makes us feel as if we are selfish. To value means that we make priority, we honor and/or find worth in ourselves. Did you hear me, we see ourselves as worthy to be invested into.

Embodying Your Extraordinary has everything to do with becoming the vessel that God has ordained for us to be. As spirit filled believers, we are to be glory carriers. We become little gods in the earth. Meaning we demonstrate his essence, nature and character. This is a posture and an authority that spirit filled believers walk in. We are not our own, but we are children of the most High God. We are called by God and have been given dominion over every living thing. The bible says it best, The heavens belongs to the Lord, but the earth he gave to the children of men. When we embody our extraordinary we walk with a level of authority that can only be obtained through our submission and surrender unto to God. As we humble ourselves, our heavenly father exalts us. To be exalted, is to embody the extraordinary. To embody means to be an expression of or give a tangible or visible form to an idea, quality, or feeling. Do you see this, when we embody we take on Gods nature. You can not take on the nature of God and not walk in the authority that God possesses.

This powerful acronym is supernatural, birthed from a supposedly natural phrase this little girl from New York and Baltimore City, would whisper to herself at the most difficult time. However, could it be that it was God keeping me.

I have named this companion to the book Courage to M.O.V.E., the Journeybook. I call it the journeybook, because I believe that God uses every experience to develop and cultivate us into the men and women that he has called us to be. Journey is defined by Oxford language as, "an act of traveling from one place to another." As you are reading this book, I want you to make a commitment to go deeper. Deeper in your relationship with God and self. Deeper in your commitment to achieving your dreams and goals and finally deeper in your ability to be courageous and resilient. I challenge you to never allow your fears, failures and frailties to prevent you from pursuing purpose.

As you go through each section, I challenge you to be reflective and introspective by being honest with yourself and willing to be accountable for each answer. This journeybook is not created to cause guilt and condemnation, but it is to bring truth and triumph in every aspect of your lives. To journey requires movement. I charge you to MOVE. I charge you to commit to overcoming every obstacle in your life, I charge you to slay the giants that have blocked your vision and finally I charge you to walk in the authority and assignment that God ordained while you were yet in your mothers womb.

Through this journeybook, you will face truths that will bring you to a place of self discovery and enlightenment. I believe that as you answer the questions and ponder upon God's word, you will be introduced to God's magnificent creation and gift, "called you." I want you to take your time traveling through the sections of this journeybook. You may even want to revisit sections after you have completed just to see yourself. It's time to go DEEPER.

Yes, Man of God, Yes Woman of God, go deep!!!

Part I

Ground Zero....Matters of the Mind!!!

Your inner thought life, provides context for your outer experiences.

A. My Thought Life

> "Casting down imaginations, and every high thing that exalteth itself against the knowledge of God, and bringing into captivity every thought to the obedience of Christ" (2 Corinthians 10:5 KJV)

When we think about our thought lives, it requires us to really be honest about what guides us. Our thought lives is what informs our perception and it is the way that we experience life. To determine the way in which you experience life, you must examine your reasoning, resistance, relationships, rituals and resources. All of these areas form your values, belief systems and the way in which we see the world.

As you complete this section, I challenge you to be introspective. According to Oxford Languages, introspection is defined as the examination or observation of one's mental and emotional processes. True introspection can only take place, when a person is willing to go beyond the defense mechanisms they have created to protect themselves from truth. We often create these defense mechanisms to help us live through difficult and painful realities. It is only through introspection and authenticity that we are able to experience truth.

Think about it, has it been difficult for you to practice introspection? Are you able to do this without getting stuck in condemnation and guilt. Are you able to honestly see your motive and behavior patterns and how they impact others?

Can you see the power in being reflective and introspective? Can you imagine the glory that will be revealed in and through our lives as you set an intention to be honest, humble and courageous in this area. I believe that as you grow in introspection, you will experience transformation and you will demonstrate the essence, nature and the Glory of God daily.

I want you to begin to see yourself through the eyes of God. We are able to see ourselves through the eyes of God through our personal and intimate relationship with God and his word. The bible says in Hebrews 4:12, *"For the word of God is living and active and full of power [making it operative, energizing, and effective]. It is sharper than any two-edged [a]sword, penetrating as far as the division of the [b]soul and spirit [the completeness of a person], and of both joints and marrow [the deepest parts of our nature], exposing and judging the very thoughts and intentions of the heart."* When we study the word it enables a person that is open to see aspects of themselves that they are unable to on their own. As spirit filled believers it is so important that we gain mastery in this area by embracing the word of God

As you begin to reflect upon the questions in this section, I challenge you to be prayerful and open to what will be revealed.

Alright, lets dive in:

1 What do you think about most?

_____
_____
_____
_____

2 Are your thoughts more negative or positive?

_____
_____
_____
_____

3 Are your thoughts faith filled or fear filled?

_____
_____
_____
_____
_____

4 What influences your thought life?

_____
_____
_____
_____
_____

5 What barriers in your thinking process, hinders you from succeeding in life?

_____
_____
_____
_____
_____

6 Is it difficult for you to let things go? Yes or no, and why?

_____
_____
_____
_____
_____

7 Do you find that you get stuck in your head easily? Do you have tunnel vision? If yes, how has it affected your life?

_____
_____
_____
_____
_____

8 Are you open or closed minded? Why? Are you rigid in your thinking?

_____
_____
_____
_____
_____

9 Is it hard for you to come to a decision? If yes, why?

_____
_____
_____
_____

10 Are you often unsure and/or doubtful?

_____
_____
_____
_____

11 Do you trust your judgement?

_____
_____
_____
_____

You made it to the end. I APPLAUD YOU!!!

My prayer that is that you gave yourself permission to be authentic and that you were able to identify patterns of thinking that need changing to enable you to live a life of freedom.

Before you go to the next chapter, I want you to begin to establish new patterns of thinking that will govern your daily life. Establishing new patterns will require reconditioning, renewal, and reinforcement. Reconditioning is defined by Oxford language as an overhaul or repair.

It is essential to repair the thought patterns that have negatively impacted your lives and relationships and you must be willing to replace with new ones. Replacement has to do with renewal. In Ephesians 4:23(AMP) the bible says, "and be continually renewed in the spirit of your mind [having a fresh, untarnished mental and spiritual attitude]" To renew your mind, requires intentionality in gaining a new perspective and perception that aligns with the Word of God. Alignment is key because it gives you a new frame of reference and way to filter your thoughts. As a spirit filled believer, our goal should always be to reflect his essence and nature and in order for us to do that, it will require alignment. Finally, reinforcement means to establish a belief or pattern of behavior. This will require daily practice so that your convictions deepen and it becomes a way of life and part of who you are.

Below I have created a space to write down positive thought patterns to incorporate into your every day life. I want you to begin to create affirmations to study daily, to help shape your thought life. These affirmations can be scriptures, inspirational quotes and/or encouraging words that replace negative thought patterns.

Changing my thoughts:

_____
_____
_____
_____
_____
_____
_____
_____

Daily Affirmation that I will live by:

_____
_____
_____
_____
_____
_____
_____
_____

B. Love

> "Thou shalt love the Lord thy God with all thy heart, and with all thy soul, and with all thy mind. "This is the first and great commandment. "And the second is like unto it, Thou shalt love thy neighbour as thyself" (Matthew 22:37–39)

In this scripture God gives his people a command to love with their hearts, mind and will. To do this it requires that we renew our mind daily through an intimate and personal relationship with God. We learn how to cultivate our love for God. As you have read in this chapter, your ability to love self and God determines your quality of life and your worldview determines the perception of your circumstances.

As you reflect upon this chapter, I want you to begin to take a deep dive of your love for God and your self. We often declare that we love God, ourselves, and others but find it difficult to express and/or put into words. I want you to take a deep dive into how love is demonstrated in your relationship with God, yourself, and others.

Taking a deep dive, simply means to take a thorough look at your ability to love, your perception of what love is and how you have been able to demonstrate love with others. This examination, will require you to be honest with yourself on a level that you may have not done before.

1 What is Love?

_____
_____
_____
_____
_____

2 Do you know what it feels like to be loved by someone else? Explain?

_____
_____
_____
_____
_____

3 Do you Love God? If so, how do you know? Is it demonstrated in your everyday life?

_____
_____
_____
_____
_____

4 Do you Love yourself? If so or not, why?

_____
_____
_____
_____
_____

5 What trauma or tragedy mostly shaped your view of you? What did this experience teach you about you, now and/or then?

_____
_____
_____
_____
_____

6 Are you unforgiving of your choices and mistakes? Do you believe in self grace and what does it mean to you? Yes or no, if yes, why?

_____
_____
_____
_____
_____

7 Do you think that you deserve God's love? Why or why not?

_____
_____
_____
_____
_____

8 Do you believe that God has set you FREE? What does being free mean to you?

_____
_____
_____
_____
_____

9 How do you show up in relationships?

_____
_____
_____
_____
_____

10 Do you find it difficult to trust? Yes or No? Why?

_____
_____
_____
_____
_____

11 Do you set boundaries in your personal, spiritual and professional life? If no, why? If yes, what are they?

_____
_____
_____
_____
_____

12 Do you have a grateful heart? Yes or no, and why? Is Gratitude a daily practice?

_____
_____
_____
_____
_____

C. Self-Care

Learning to take care of yourself is one of the most important components of your journey through purpose. Most people are accustomed to taking care of everyone else while not making themselves a priority. Making yourself a priority is not about being selfish as much as it is about learning to preserve you so that you are able to function as the best version of yourself daily.

In this section, I want you to challenge yourself to reflect upon your daily life and examine whether self care is apart of your everyday practice. How good are you to you?

Now before you begin your reflection, I want to remind you of the Acronym, VITALS used in the book. I want to highlight this because, it is imperative that you check your V.I.T.A.L.S. periodically to ensure that self care is a priority. Remember each of us should have a self-care survival tool box.

Value your personal needs – Take care of your emotional and mental well-being. You matter. The Bible says in III John 2 (AMP), *"Beloved, I pray that in every way you may succeed and prosper and be in good health [physically], just as [I know] your soul prospers [spiritually]."* Allow yourself to feel and to be able to articulate what you are feeling. Know that God desires for your soul to be free. Don't suppress your emotions or avoid dealing with them because of fear of what others will think. Give yourself permission to experience positive and negative emotions. Learn how to manage them well. Do not put the happiness of others before your own. Avoid being a people pleaser or a busy body.

Invest time and care in you – Invest in your physical, mental, and emotional health. Make sure you attend annual checkups and address physical symptoms that are out of the norm. Make healthy food choices and monitor your intake of unhealthy choices. Exercise and get the proper rest needed. Remember that God wants you to take care of yourself and not to work yourself to exhaustion – consider Psalm 127:2 (AMP): *"It is vain for you to rise early, to retire late, to eat the bread of anxious labors—for He gives [blessings] to His beloved even in his* *sleep."* You do not have to burn yourself out in labor to receive the blessings of God. Make every effort not to overwork yourself.

Time – Respect your time. Learn how to balance personal care, relationships, work productivity, silence, and rest. Don't allow people to intrude upon your time or make commitments for you. What do you spend most of your time doing? Monitor what you spend your time on and whether or not it is healthy for you. There are times in our lives where silence is necessary and is also a part of our self care. When we don't see silence as a powerful force, we run the risk of living noisy lives and creating distractions that rob us of time and peace.

Associations – Monitor your associations. Avoid toxic and unhealthy relationships. Know when to say no to yourself and others. Don't let people suck the life out of you. Learn to preserve your energy by being selective of whom you show up for and when. Know that another person's crisis may not be yours. Avoid being an enabler and doing for others what they can do for themselves.

Live – Allow yourself to live and enjoy life. Seek out hobbies, things that you love to do. Smile often. The Bible says in Proverbs 17:22 (AMP), *"A happy heart is good medicine and a joyful mind causes healing, but a broken spirit dries up the bones."* Practice daily gratitude. Stop waiting to find happiness and actively choose it instead. Have knowledge of what you want in life and don't mind pursuing. Avoid living in regret. John 10:10 (AMP) says, *"The thief comes only in order to steal and kill and destroy. I came that they may have and enjoy life, and have it in abundance [to the full, till it overflows]."* When we fail to experience joy and this abundant life, we are being robbed of the blessing of God. Let's get into the practice of being intentional with our mental health.

Set boundaries – Caring for ourselves also involves our ability to set healthy boundaries in our lives with others and their affairs. Pursue peace. Try not to worry about things that you cannot change. Choose to live in the moment. Learn the art of forgiveness and letting go.

In Chapter 3, there is a section on setting boundaries. This section is so important because it helps bring clarity as to why setting boundaries is connected to the concept of self care. It says, **"Emotional and intellectual boundaries protect your self esteem and it gives you the ability to separate your feelings from others."** (pg 32) Separating your feelings from that of others is important because we often are consumed with the needs of others so much so that our needs are placed on the back burner. We spend a great deal of time making things happen for others and being black mailed by the idea of hurting other peoples feelings, that we compromise our own." Does this sound familiar?

Now it's time for you to create and fill your self care tool box. I want you to think about what things in your life are energy depleters, peace blockers, and most of all distractions. Begin to map your self care plan. People often see self care as going to spas, getting nails done, exercising, getting haircuts and/or new hairstyles, etc. Those things can be a part of self care, but how many of you know, you can find yourself in the chair getting a hair cut or getting your nails done, still being tormented with no rest. I hope you understand what I am saying. Self care also has to do with you allowing yourself to "Be" by embracing you and teaching yourself to live authentically, protecting your energy and personal space. It's about being intentional and making yourself priority. This may take some time, however I challenge you to start. Your journey through purpose will only get better as you make "YOU" more of a priority.

Self Care Toolbox

Part II

The Motivation to M.O.V.E

You are <u>braver</u> than you believe, <u>stronger</u> than you seem, <u>smarter</u> than you think

by Christopher Robbin (A.A.Milne)

In this section of the book, the reader is given a guide as to how to move forward as they journey through purpose. Having motivation to move forward is essential and requires the effort of every individual to cultivate and maintain. Motivation is defined by Oxford Languages as the general desire or willingness of someone to do something. Motivation can be seen as the fuel we need to get through our challenges, triumphs and trials. It is that one thing that helps us to accomplish what is set before you.

According to the book, Action is what makes all the difference between who we want to be and who we become. Action has a lot to do what what we say and what we do. As you reflect upon this section of the book, I want you to begin to hold yourself accountable and think on what will it take to get you to that place of action in your life. What is the language that guides you as you pursue your purpose. Our language can produce action if we give ourselves permission to follow through. Now I do not know what action looks like for you, but you do. Begin to reflect upon the assignment and purpose of God for your life, and M.O.V.E.

1 Do you believe that you are consistent in your pursuit to grow? Why or why not?

_____
_____
_____
_____
_____
_____

2 What is your greatest fear in life?

_____
_____
_____
_____
_____
_____

3 What do you think this fear has robbed you of?

_____
_____
_____
_____
_____
_____

4 What prevents you from taking action in your life when it comes to the pursuit of your purpose?

_____
_____
_____
_____
_____
_____

5 What does courage mean to you? Do you possess, why or why not?

_____
_____
_____
_____
_____
_____

6 Do you seek God for direction, when pursuing your purpose? What does this look like for you?

_____
_____
_____
_____
_____
_____

7 When you experience failure and/or setbacks, is it difficult for you to bounce back, or do you find yourself stuck? If yes, why?

_____
_____
_____
_____
_____
_____

8 Do you see yourself as a leader? If so, why? What makes you a leader?

_____
_____
_____
_____
_____
_____

9 How courageous are you in your communication? What is the language that guides you to action? or in-action?

_____
_____
_____
_____
_____
_____

10 How willing are you to have difficult and authentic conversations, when pursuing purpose with yourself and others?

_____
_____
_____
_____
_____
_____

11 In your communication, do you lead with your head or your heart? How has this worked out for you in your journey through purpose?

_____
_____
_____
_____
_____
_____

12 Have you sought God concerning your purpose? If yes, have you been able to hear him concerning your purpose?

_____
_____
_____
_____
_____
_____

13 Do you know your purpose? If, yes what is it? If no, what do you think is the hindrance in identifying?

_____
_____
_____
_____
_____
_____

14 Do you have the capacity to see what God sees concerning you and his purpose for your life?

_____
_____
_____
_____
_____
_____

15 What has God shown you regarding your purpose and if so, are you willing to obey?

_____
_____
_____
_____
_____
_____
_____
_____
_____
_____

This section will challenge the reader to pursue God concerning their purpose. It is essential that as spirit filled believers, you are willing to allow the Lord to direct your paths. This requires a level of submission and surrender that you may have been unwilling to yield to. Pursuing your purpose and being activated in it fully, will require your constant pursuit of the presence of God in your life. Matthews 6:33(AMP) says, *"But first and most importantly seek (aim at, strive after) His kingdom and His righteousness [His way of doing and being right—the attitude and character of God], and all these things will be given to you also."*

As spirit filled believers we must be willing to do things Gods way for in this we experience fulfillment in all of our endeavors. You must trust that God knows just what you need in all things. As you complete this section, I challenge you to establish a consistent prayer life and take time to read the word of God daily. It is also good to begin to journal what you hear when you seek the Lord. Journaling enables you to document what you hear in your time of prayer, but also your thoughts and intentions concerning what you hear in that moment. Journaling helps a person to remain present.

PART III

THE MANDATE TO M.O.V.E

THE MANDATE IS CLEAR, GOD'S NATURE MUST BE REFLECTED ON EARTH

by SUNDAY ADELAJA

The Mandate to MOVE is crucial as you journey through purpose because it is crucial to execute that which we have discovered. To be honest discovering your purpose, understanding your spiritual gifts and embracing how God has uniquely created you can be a very intimidating experience. One that often paralyzes you with fear and leads to the question, am I enough? My prayer is that the last 2 sections has helped you to face these thoughts head on and to replace them with the Truth of God's Word concerning you and your purpose. Once you have embraced your uniqueness, its time to execute.

This section has the particular focus on Mandate. According to Oxford Languages, Mandate means that you have been given the authority to carry out a course of action. Did you hear that? You have been given the authority to carry out your assignment, your purpose!!!

In this section, I talked about the birthing process and the importance of creating the environment for birthing to take place. It's time for your delivery. I want you to begin to ask yourself some really challenging questions regarding the hindrances to execution. This will require you to be reflective and honest. The good thing about this Journeybook is no one has to see it but you. I want you to begin to free yourself of the internal weights and thoughts that so easily beset you and that prevent you from discovering and fulfilling your purpose.

The bible says in Proverbs 29:18(MSG), *"If people can't see what God is doing, they stumble all over themselves; but when they <u>attend</u> to what he reveals they are most blessed."* It is time to ATTEND to what God has revealed. God has spoken to you regarding your direction, regarding your purpose and it is time for you to attend to what he has spoken. Attending to what God has revealed requires the elimination of excuses and the demonstration of discipline, grit, and follow-through. It's time to EXECUTE!!!

Are you disciplined as it relates to your spiritual life? If yes......................., please write down characteristics that you exhibit that keep you focused and consistent in your purpose. If no......................, Please explain why?

_____
_____
_____
_____
_____
_____
_____
_____

Do you typically take action, once you know to do something or do you wait to be given permission to do so? Yes .... No .... What typically motivates you to take action? Please explain why?

_____
_____
_____
_____
_____
_____
_____
_____

Do you have thoughts of inferiority and/or insecurity that rob you of your movement in purpose? Yes .... No .... If yes, what are they?

_____

_____

_____

_____

_____

_____

_____

_____

_____

Do you ever feel unworthy of God using you as his vessel of honor? Yes .... No .... if yes, does this stop you from M.O.V.E.ing? Please explain.

How is your prayer life? Do you set aside time to pray daily and/or often? Yes .... No .... Do you believe that God hears your prayers?

___

Do you believe in you? Yes .... No ....Please explain why, whether you select yes or no.

___

Do you play it safe or are you a risk taker? Do you think outside the box or are you willing to do things that you have never done before? Do you make excuses for not allowing yourself to try something new? Are you uncomfortable with the unfamiliar?

_____
_____
_____
_____
_____
_____
_____
_____

Do you value your voice or do you see yourself as invisible? Have you ever struggled with the fear of rejection and if so, has it hindered you from executing your purpose? Yes.............. No............. Whether you select yes or no, please explain?

_____
_____
_____
_____
_____
_____
_____
_____

Do you struggle with procrastination? Is it difficult for you to get started and remain consistent? Do you follow through on what you say you will do? A great deal of people, often have two answers to these questions in terms of what is done for others and what is done for self. As you answer, I want you to focus on YOU!!!

_____
_____
_____
_____
_____
_____
_____
_____
_____

Are you a good steward of your time or are you wasteful? If you could survey your time, what do you spend most of your time on, outside of work? Do you find that most of your time is spent doing things for others? Yes .... No............... Does it interfere with doing what God has called you to do?

_____
_____
_____
_____
_____
_____
_____

What are the time wasters, energy depleters and/or distractions in your life that hinder you from discovering and executing your purpose? I want you to begin to examine the fruitless activities that robs you of your time. Remember this requires authenticity and truth regarding you.

_____
_____
_____
_____
_____
_____
_____
_____

Do you struggle with gaining direction in your purpose? Yes .... No..............
If yes, explain?

_____
_____
_____
_____
_____
_____
_____

You made it through this section. Now I know there was some tough areas in this section that required deep thought. I want you to continue pondering upon these questions and as you continue to journey through purpose, answer them. The discovery and execution of your purpose is a journey that will evolve over a lifetime. Purpose is not a destination, it is a journey. It is crucial that you learn to be patient, giving yourself the grace to grow. Giving yourself grace to grow requires the avoidance of regrets, refusing to condemn yourself for the things in which you have allowed, and learning to live beyond what you cannot control.

My prayer is that this Journeybook has facilitated a process of introspection and reflection that produces transformation in your life. Remember its all about the journey. It's time to M.O.V.E..

www.ingramcontent.com/pod-product-compliance
Lightning Source LLC
Chambersburg PA
CBHW081128080526
44587CB00021B/3799